Earnings Inequality

Earnings Inequality

The Influence of Changing Opportunities and Choices

Robert H. Haveman

The AEI Press

Publisher for the American Enterprise Institute
WASHINGTON, D.C.

1996

Support for this research from the Jerome Levy Institute of Bard College, the Institute for Research on Poverty at the University of Wisconsin-Madison, the Robert M. LaFollette Institute of Public Affairs, and the American Enterprise Institute is gratefully acknowledged. Many of the estimates described in this volume were prepared in collaboration with Lawrence Baron.

To order call toll free 1-800-462-6420 or 1-717-794-3800. For all other inquiries please contact the AEI Press, 1150 Seventeenth Street, N.W., Washington, D.C. 20036 or call 1-800-862-5801.

ISBN 0-8447-7076-0

1   3   5   7   9   10   8   6   4   2

The AEI Press
Publisher for the American Enterprise Institute
1150 17th Street, N.W., Washington, D.C. 20036

ISBN 978-0-8447-7076-5

Contents

Foreword

This study is one of a series commissioned by the American Enterprise Institute on trends in the level and distribution of U.S. wages, income, wealth, consumption, and other measures of material welfare. The issues addressed in the series involve much more than dry statistics: they touch on fundamental aspirations of the American people—material progress, widely shared prosperity, and just reward for individual effort—and affect popular understanding of the successes and shortcomings of the private market economy and of particular government policies. For these reasons, discussions of "economic inequality" in the media and political debate are often partial and partisan as well as superficial. The AEI series is intended to improve the public discussion by bringing new data to light, exploring the strengths and weaknesses of various measures of economic welfare, and highlighting important questions of interpretations, causation, and consequence.

Each study in the series is presented and discussed in draft form at an AEI seminar prior to publication by the AEI Press. Marvin Kosters, director of economic policy studies at AEI, organized the series and moderated the seminars. A current list of published studies appears on the last page.

CHRISTOPHER DEMUTH
President, American Enterprise Institute

1
Introduction

Earnings inequality among working-age males in the United States has increased rapidly since the early 1970s. Several studies have documented these changes and have also sought to apportion the increase among several plausible factors. A variety of potentially causal factors have been identified, including:

- growing "internationalization" of the economy and the changed trade patterns that this implies
- growing skill disparities in spite of narrowing educational differences
- changes in the industrial pattern of labor demand from the union-protected manufacturing sector to the service sector
- the reduction in the size and power of labor unions in traditional union-protected sectors
- the growing disparity in skill demands in the service sector, ranging from high and rising skill needs in the technology-based sectors to low and perhaps declining skill requirements in the recreation, restaurant, and personal service sectors
- changes in the demographic structure of the work force, such as age (experience) and ethnic distribution

Although different analysts assign different weights to these factors, evidence supports attributing some of the rise in inequality to growth in skill disparities within schooling and experience groups. Shifts in labor demand from manufacturing to services (and in the service sector

1

toward both ends of the skill distribution), as well as business sector "downsizing" and restructuring, have also been cited as sources of growing earnings disparity in some recent analyses, but evidence on these causes is somewhat mixed. Although much of the growth in male earnings inequality is a result of changes within schooling and experience groups, increases in the returns to schooling and age (experience) have also contributed to the increase in earnings disparities.

At the same time that analysts have attempted to attribute the growth in earnings inequality to these various supply- and demand-side sources, a second discussion regarding the sources of the growing inequality has been taking place. The question here concerns the extent to which the growth in earnings inequality has been "voluntary" or "structural"; whether it stems from changes in people's "choices" or in the "opportunities" that they encounter.

In this analysis I first describe the difficult challenge of empirically distinguishing changes in the distribution of earnings that are due to changes in opportunities from those that result from voluntary choices. Then I discuss several studies that have attempted to attribute the observed change in male earnings inequality since the early 1970s to changes in the inequality of the distribution of wage rates (which are commonly thought of as reflecting "opportunities") and changes in the inequality of hours worked (presumed to reflect "choices"). I summarize the conclusion reached by the authors of these studies—namely, that the increase in the inequality of wage rates rather than working time accounts for virtually all the increase in earnings inequality—and identify some important concerns about this conclusion.

The next two sections present and discuss the results of an analysis done within the statistical framework of the prior studies but which attempts to correct for one of the more serious shortcomings of the earlier studies, namely, the "noisy" estimate of the wage rate on which their results rest. I find that changes in inequality of work time account for more of the change in earnings inequality than other studies suggest. I analyze the beginning and ending dates of the periods during which changes in earnings inequality have been measured and conclude that the evidence on the dominant role of changes in the inequality of wage rates, or opportunities, depends on the specific time period from which the data are taken. Finally, I present further evidence on the role played by the changing distribution of employment according to work pattern—as between, say, full-time, year-round (FTYR) work; part-time work; part-year work; and joblessness—in explaining the growth in earnings inequality.

2
"Opportunity" versus "Choice"

S eparating voluntary from structural sources of growing inequality is devilishly difficult. In a market
economy, observed outcomes at a point in time pre-
sumably reflect an equilibrium in which individuals have
made choices that will maximize their well-being, subject
to their tastes and preferences and the opportunities
available at that time. An individual's wage rate and
hours worked—and hence, earnings—represent this
equilibrium. The distribution of wage rates, hours
worked, and individual earnings at a point in time is the
aggregation of all these equilibrium outcomes.

The distribution of these values at a later point in
time reflects a new set of equilibrium outcomes. Outcomes change because of complex and interdependent
shifts in both labor demand and labor supply conditions
over time. As a result of these shifts, we observe changes
in wage rates, employment levels, and work time; they
lead to the equilibrium outcomes that reflect these new
conditions. These labor demand and labor supply shifts
and the resulting new equilibrium outcomes, in turn, de-
rive from still more fundamental changes in technology,
tastes and preferences, and a wide variety of other factors
that are held constant when analyzing the equilibrium in
a particular market at a particular point in time. Taken
together, changes in these factors determine whether the

earnings distribution has become more or less unequal over time.

These market changes affect individual workers, and together with changes in their tastes, preferences, or needs, determine whether we observe a change in an individual's wage rate or work pattern (full-time work, part-time work, or no work at all). Hence, while changes in work opportunities and tastes for work underlie, and cause, some of the changes in individual work patterns and wage rates, it is problematic to assign responsibility for any observed change in wage rate, hours worked, or earnings to either a change in the individual's voluntary "choices" or a change in the structural "opportunities" that he or she confronts. Similarly, attributing responsibility for, say, an increase in the variation of earnings among a group of people to changes in "choices" or changes in "opportunities" is not straightforward. If for no other reason, such assignment ignores the fact that the changes in wage rates, employment levels, working times, and earnings themselves depend upon choices that are made in response to the opportunities that are available in an interdependent, general equilibrium world.

Still, the question of the relative role of changing opportunities (taken to be imposed by the structure of the economy) or changing choices (taken to be voluntary) in accounting for an observed increase in earnings inequality is an interesting and important one. The approach taken by researchers in studying this issue follows from the standard economist's model of the labor-leisure choice: a rational individual chooses his or her level of working time, given a budget constraint reflecting available wage rate opportunities. The empirical procedure involves allocating the observed change in earnings inequality from t to $t + 1$ to either the change in *wage rate* inequality from t to $t + 1$ (interpreted as reflecting altered opportunities) or the change in the inequality of *hours worked* (reflecting changed choices).[1] The implicit notion is that workers are able to secure a full-time job at their observed wage rate if they so desire; any deviation from that norm represents a voluntary work-time choice.[2]

This approach, of course, takes a huge leap from the standard, partial equilibrium labor supply model to the general equilibrium world of changing earnings distributions.

Consider the following examples of employment changes of prototypical workers from t to $t + 1$; each change tends to increase inequality in the distribution of earnings. In each case, I describe the plausible contributions of changed "choices" and changed "opportunities" to the increase in inequality and then the allocation to these two categories that results from application of the common empirical procedure; in several cases, the plausible explanation of the allocation diverges from the assignment made by the standard procedure.[3]

• A fifty-one-year-old male factory manager earning $100,000 in year t is permanently laid off because the plant is closed; he is not able to find a managerial job and is observed jobless and with zero earnings in year $t + 1$.

Does this earnings change seem to be due to a change in opportunities or to a change in choices? Surely, the manager could find work at, say, $30,000 per year, so some part of the earnings change is due to choice. With growth from t to $t + 1$ in the number of displaced workers with managerial skills, however, the changed structure of opportunities also plays a role.

The standard empirical approach allocates changes in earnings inequality between changes in hours-worked inequality and changes in wage rate inequality *among workers*. Hence, it would fail to include this observation in the analysis because in year $t + 1$ the person is a nonworker.

• In year t, a full-time worker earning $30,000 per year in a manufacturing plant is laid off when his company "downsizes." In year $t + 1$, the worker has a part-time job earning the same wage rate; his annual earnings have fallen to $17,000. Although the worker could have obtained another full-time job at a lower wage rate, which would have yielded earnings in excess of $17,000, he chose the part-time job.

Again, do changed choices or changed opportunities account for the earnings change? In this case the worker sacrificed hours of work to maintain his wage rate. Although the layoff reflects a reduction in opportunities and therefore accounts for the job change, the worker chose fewer hours at a higher wage rate over more hours at a lower wage rate. A reasonable interpretation would, perhaps, allocate a portion of the earnings change to voluntary choice and a portion to changed opportunity.

The standard empirical approach would attribute the resulting increase in earnings inequality entirely to choice, because the change in earnings is matched by a change in hours worked and the observed wage rate is unchanged.

• A full-time worker earning $45,000 per year takes a job paying somewhat less than his prior, above-average wage rate, but one that allows him to work overtime. In his new job, his earnings in year $t + 1$ are $55,000 per year.

Because of this change, earnings inequality increases; however, wage rate inequality decreases, and hours-worked inequality increases. Does the disequalizing earnings change seem to be due to a change in voluntary choices or to a change in opportunities? In this case, both the wage rate change and the hours-worked change would appear to reflect a voluntary choice.

The standard empirical approach would yield a different allocation. While the wage rate decrease tends to reduce inequality in the distribution of wage rates, the change in hours worked increases the dispersion in the distribution of hours worked. In this case, *more than 100 percent* of the resulting increase in earnings inequality would be attributed to choice.

• A delivery truck driver earning $24,000 per year is promoted, and as a result his below-average wage rate increases. His earnings rise to $30,000. His working time per week does not change.

In this case, the increase in earnings would seem to be a response to a change in opportunities. The standard empirical approach would attribute the change in earnings inequality to an increase in the wage rate (with no change in hours worked or voluntary choice). However, in this case the increase in the observed wage rate *decreases* the inequality in the distribution of earnings; the worker's wage rate moves closer to the mean.

These examples make clear the difficulty of distinguishing and statistically attributing the relative contributions of opportunity changes and changes in voluntary choice to any observed change in earnings inequality.

3
Changing Inequality of Male Earnings

In recent years, a large number of studies have attempted to document—and to sort out the causes of—changes in the distribution of male earnings, wage rates, and hours worked (see Levy and Murnane 1992 for a review). Here, I focus on studies that have measured the changes in inequality using the variance in the logarithm (VLN) measure of inequality, a standard empirical measure that separates the increase in inequality into its wage rate and hours components. Table 3-1 summarizes some of the findings of these studies.

An important study in this set is Burtless's 1990 paper "Earnings Inequality over the Business and Demographic Cycles." Burtless uses a sample of wage and salary workers from the March Current Population Survey (CPS) to document the long-term (1947–1986) trend of rising earnings inequality and finds that during the 1980s earnings inequality accelerated, especially for full-time, year-round workers.[4] He also analyzes the contribution to earnings inequality of changes in wage rate inequality (a variable obtained by dividing earnings in the year by the product of weeks worked and "usual" weekly hours worked) and changes in variables reflecting inequality in work time.[5]

Burtless finds the VLN of earnings in his sample of males to have risen from about 1.30 in 1973 to about 1.55 in 1987, an increase of about .25. He attributes about 75

TABLE 3-1
Variance of Logarithm (VLN) and Change in VLN of Male Earnings from Various Studies, 1973 to Late 1980s

	Burtless[a]	Moffitt[b]	Moffitt[c]	Karoly[d]	Bluestone[e]	Juhn, Murphy, Pierce[f]	Blackburn[g]
All earners							
1973	1.30	1.25	1.48	1.36	1.40		
1987	1.55	1.61	1.44	1.53	1.64		
Absolute change	+.25	+.36	−.04	+.17	+.24		
Percentage change	+19.2	+28.8	−2.7	+12.5	+17.1		
FTYR earners							
1973						.50	.25
1985						.59	.32
Absolute change						+.09	+.07
Percentage change						+17.9	+29.7

a. Wage and salary earnings plus self-employment income for males aged sixteen and older with positive wage and salary earnings greater than their self-employment income. The top 2 percent of the distribution are excluded. Estimates from graphs in Burtless 1990, p. 111.

b. Wage and salary earnings for white males aged sixteen to sixty-one with positive earnings who report less than seventy hours of work a week. Square of standard errors reported in Moffitt 1990, table 1, p. 203.

c. Wage and salary earnings for black males aged sixteen to sixty-one with positive earnings who report less than seventy hours of work a week. Square of standard errors reported in Moffitt 1990, table 1, p. 203.

d. Wage and salary earnings for males aged sixteen and older with positive wage and salary earnings (Karoly 1988).

e. Wage and salary earnings for males aged sixteen and older with positive wage and salary earnings (Bluestone 1989).

f. Weekly wages of white males who worked at least thirty-five hours in each week they worked (Juhn, Murphy, and Pierce 1989).

g. Wage and salary earnings for white males aged eighteen to sixty-five with no self-employment income who worked more than thirty-four hours a week for at least fifty weeks. Workers in agriculture, private household service, and welfare and religious services, and all other workers with earnings less than $2,080 (1984 dollars), are excluded.

SOURCE: Blackburn 1990, table 1, p. 446.

percent of this increase (about .19 of the .25) to an increase in the variance of the logarithm of the wage rate. About −.025 of the increase is attributed to a *decrease* in the variance of the logarithm of weeks worked, about −.003 is attributed to a *decrease* in the variance of the logarithm of hours worked, and about .090 is attributed to an increase in the variance of the combination of covariance terms. The sum of those values—+.190, −.025, −.003, and +.090—about equals the increase in the VLN of earnings of +.250. Clearly, the increase in inequality of his measure of the wage rate accounts for the overwhelming bulk of the increase in earnings inequality.

Moffitt (1990) also provides evidence on the relative contributions of changes in wage rate and hours-worked inequality to increasing earnings inequality. Using data from the March CPS, Moffitt concludes that the increase in earnings inequality among black and white males from 1967 to 1987 is due only to an increase in wage rate inequality and not to an increase in inequality of hours worked. Indeed, for white males he finds that the variance in the distribution of the logarithm of annual hours worked *falls* from 1973 to 1987 (pp. 215–17). Like Burtless, Moffitt uses March CPS data and is constrained by having to work with very noisy measures of hours worked.[6]

Karoly (1992) also presents evidence of the increases in weekly and hourly wage inequality for both all male wage and salary workers and all FTYR male workers by looking at changes in selected percentiles of the distribution relative to the median. While the implied increase in the inequality of the calculated wage rate for all workers exceeds that for FTYR workers, the extent of the increase in inequality between the two groups does not appear to differ substantially. She finds that wage rate inequality is growing almost as fast among FTYR workers as among all workers and that hourly and weekly wage inequalities are growing as well as annual earnings inequality. She therefore concludes that "most of the increase in inequality in annual wage and salary income since the late 1970s is the result of an increase in inequality in hourly wages and not simply greater variance in weeks or hours worked" (p. 51).[7]

In sum, these studies indicate that from the early 1970s to the late 1980s there has been:

* a substantial increase in the VLN of earnings for all male workers, ranging from about .17 (Karoly) to .25 (Burtless), depending on the sample of males and the definition of earnings
* a sizable increase in the VLN of the wage rate of about .19 (Burtless), again depending on the sample and the measurement of the wage rate
* a substantially smaller increase in the VLN of earnings or wages of FTYR workers, ranging from about .07 (Blackburn) to about .09 (Juhn, Murphy, and Pierce)
* a *decrease* in the VLN of work time (hours worked per year; weeks worked per year), ranging from about − .03 (Burtless) to about − .09 (Moffitt)

Although these research results are revealing, they leave a number of questions unanswered. First, how reliable are these decomposition estimates, given that the estimates of hours worked, and hence the wage-rate estimates, calculated from March CPS data are weak, noisy, and precarious? As has been indicated, using these estimates, one is likely to overstate the increase in inequality attributed to increases in wage rate dispersion, taken to reflect changes in opportunities. Second, do these results square with what one would expect from the reallocation of the male work force from FTYR jobs to jobs that provide either part-time or part-year employment? The *decrease* in the VLN of hours worked for all male workers, as suggested by Moffitt's results, seems inconsistent with this work-time shift. (I will return to this later.) Finally, a number of anomalies in the patterns of inequality changes in these studies make it difficult to reach any reliable assessment of the relative contributions of wage rate and hours-worked inequality changes to the general increase in earnings inequality.[8]

4
An Alternative Decomposition of Earnings Inequality

Concern about the reliability of the implications for the "opportunity" versus "choice" debate of the findings of the cited studies—in particular, their reliance on the noisy, constructed wage rate variable—suggests that an alternative approach could yield additional insights into the roles of structural and voluntary determinants of the increase in earnings inequality. Here, I summarize the results of such an approach.[9]

From the U.S. Census Bureau's Current Population Survey Public Use Files for March 1974 and March 1989, I extracted two samples of eighteen- to sixty-four-year-old males for each year. The first sample includes all males who record positive earnings and positive weeks worked in 1973 and 1988, respectively. I refer to this as the sample of "workers." The second sample includes all males aged eighteen to sixty-four and is referred to as the "all males" sample. The dates were chosen to correspond with the studies cited in table 3–1.

Table 4–1 displays the distribution of the earnings of these two samples for 1973 and 1988. Several aspects of the distributions are noteworthy. First, the real mean earnings level for both the workers and all males (in 1988 dollars) shows essentially no growth, reflecting the stagnation of individual earnings over the period 1973–1988.

TABLE 4–1
PERCENTILE DISTRIBUTION OF TOTAL EARNINGS, ALL MALES AND
MALE WORKERS AGED 18–64, 1973 AND 1988
(1988 dollars)

Percentile	Male Workers		All Males	
	1973	1988	1973	1988
1	500	400	0	0
5	2,500	2,000	0	0
10	5,000	4,400	1,600	0
20	11,200	9,200	7,500	5,000
30	15,400	13,500	13,200	10,000
40	19,900	18,000	17,800	14,800
50	23,300	22,000	22,100	19,800
60	26,800	26,000	25,300	24,500
70	30,100	31,000	29,800	30,000
80	36,300	38,000	34,800	36,000
90	45,500	50,000	44,700	48,000
95	57,100	62,100	56,600	60,000
99	99,400	100,000	99,400	100,000
Mean	25,400	25,500	23,600	22,900
VLN	1.11	1.29	2.77	3.55
Percentage change	16.2		28.2	

NOTES: Total earnings are equal to the sum of wage and salary earnings plus self-employment income. Figures are rounded to the nearest $100. Total earnings are top-coded at $99,999 in 1988 dollars. Observations weighted using March supplemental weights.
SOURCE: Author's calculations using March 1974 and 1989 CPS.

Second, for both the workers and all males, the earnings distribution in 1988 is substantially more unequal than it was in 1973. The VLN of earnings for male workers increased by .18, from 1.11 to 1.29, or by 16.2 percent. For all males, however, the increase in earnings inequality is much larger. For this population, the VLN of earnings rose by .78, from 2.77 to 3.55, or by 28.2 percent.

Finally, as seen in the distributions for all males,

the percentage of males who report no earnings or hours worked in the entire year—the jobless, as opposed to the "unemployed," which may include people who are not without work for an entire year—is substantially larger in 1988 than in 1973.[10] In 1973, 6.3 percent of working-age males (3.5 million people) were jobless; by 1988, the number of jobless increased to 6.9 million, about 9.6 percent of the working-age male population.

These data also document a substantial increase in annual male earnings inequality over the period since 1973. The sources and implications of that change, however, are unclear. Individual earnings are, after all, an annual report of labor market income and hence reflect both the wage rate earned by an individual in a particular year (w) and the amount of time worked during that period (h). Both w and h are, at least partially, chosen by the worker.[11]

The fact that individual annual earnings equal the product of a wage rate and the number of hours worked $(E_i = w_i \times h_i)$ may provide a way of understanding more fully the sources and implications of the increase in earnings inequality. If w is the payment per hour worked, reflecting (1) the skills and talents that individuals bring to the labor market (that is, their human capital); (2) the implicit market price of their human capital; (3) the characteristics of the jobs that are made available; and (4) the trade-off that the individual makes among wage rates and the other characteristics of available jobs, then, in addition to human capital characteristics, the variation in w is explained by the structure of implicit prices of human capital characteristics, the pattern of job opportunities, and the nature of individual worker choices.

Similarly, inequality in the distribution of h reflects both the distribution of individual workers' labor supply choices (reflecting their tastes and needs) and the part-time, part-year, and full-time distribution of available jobs offered by employers.

From this perspective, one possible explanation for the observed increase in annual earnings inequality would be increasing inequality in the distribution of potential human capital services possessed by the male work force. At one extreme, an increase in the inequality of human capital—schooling, work experience, age, or other factors relevant to generating labor market income—could account for the entire increase in inequality in observed earnings.[12] Conversely, the increase in annual earnings inequality could reflect only an increase in the inequality in the distribution of time worked or the utilization of human capital.[13] Alternatively, increases in the inequality of the distribution of human capital and its utilization could, together, account for the observed increase in earnings inequality. Or increases in the inequality of either human capital or its utilization could be offset by decreases in inequality of the other and, on net, yield an increase in earnings inequality.

A fundamental question, then, concerns the changes over time in the more permanent labor market capabilities that individuals possess—say, their human capital or their earnings capabilities. What has happened to the level of the potential services of the accumulated human resources possessed by the American male work force, and what has happened to the inequality in the distribution of those earnings capabilities? Focusing on this more permanent variable may offer a somewhat different, and longer-run, perspective on the sources of the increase in earnings inequality in the United States.

Using the CPS data, I have explored the level and the inequality in the underlying distribution of human capital characteristics (or potential services of human capital) and the prices associated with those characteristics; I refer to the value of these potential services as "earnings capabilities." The basic questions are:

• How did the level and the dispersion of earnings capabilities change over the 1973–1988 period?

- Did the changes in longer-term or "permanent" earnings capabilities parallel the pattern of observed changes in the distribution of shorter-term observed earnings, or did they not?
- To what extent can the pattern of increased earnings inequality be explained by changes in the distribution of earnings capabilities?

I define individual earnings capability (EC) to be the level of earnings that a person would be expected to receive if he used his skills and capabilities at their capacity (defined as the earnings of individuals with like characteristics who work full time, year round).

The underlying concept of earnings capabilities that is reflected in the EC measure needs to be clearly understood. The value of EC for an individual in a particular year—that is, his human capital in that year—is the product of his human capital characteristics and the implicit "price" that those characteristics would receive in the full-time, year-round labor market. The distribution of EC is the distribution of earnings that would result if *every* worker (or every male) secured a full-time, year-round job that reflected his human capital characteristics and the prices of these characteristics.[14]

Estimating this value requires that one (1) observe the relevant labor market–human capital characteristics of individuals; (2) measure the implicit full-time, year-round returns associated with those characteristics; and (3) calculate the total reward (earnings) that an individual would receive if he used those capabilities in the labor market to their capacity.

To estimate individual EC, and hence the distribution of EC, I used separate earnings equations for white and nonwhite FTYR workers in both 1973 and 1988. Each equation includes a selectivity correction variable calculated from a prior equation to account for the estimation of the earnings function on only workers who chose full-

TABLE 4–2
INEQUALITY OF EARNINGS AND EARNINGS CAPACITY, MALE
WORKERS AND ALL MALES AGED 18–64, 1973 AND 1988

	Earnings		Earnings Capacity		Ratio of Inequality of EC to Earnings	
	1973	1988	1973	1988	1973	1988
Male workers						
Variance of logs	1.11	1.29	.283	.349	.255	.271
Percentage change	16.2		23.3			
Absolute change	.18		.066			
All males						
Variance of logs	2.77	3.55	.287	.353	.104	.099
Percentage change	28.2		23.0			
Absolute change	.78		.066			

NOTES: People with zero or negative earnings were assigned earnings of $100 for variance of logs calculations (zero otherwise). Earnings and earnings capacity are top-coded at $99,999 in 1988 dollars. Earnings capacity has variance adjustment. Observations weighted using March supplemental weights.
SOURCE: Author's calculations using March 1974 and 1989 CPS.

time, year-round work.[15] The independent variables in the earnings equations reflect factors that are traditionally believed to determine human capital; they include education, age, region, urbanization, marital status, and number of children. The expected FTYR earnings of each individual in our two samples is calculated by using the coefficients from the appropriate earnings equation and the individual's characteristics.[16]

As is clear from table 4–2, the VLN measure of inequality indicates that the distribution of EC is less unequal than that of earnings. For workers, the ratio of the VLN of EC to the VLN of earnings is about .25 to .27.[17] (For all males, the VLN of EC is only about 10 percent of the VLN of earnings, and it fell slightly over the 1973 to

TABLE 4–3
SUMMARY MEASURES OF INEQUALITY IN CAPACITY UTILIZATION
RATES WITHOUT VARIANCE ADJUSTMENT, MALE WORKERS AND
ALL MALES AGED 18–64, 1973 AND 1988

	Male Workers		All Males	
	1973	1988	1973	1988
Variance of logs	.89	.99	2.48	3.18
Percentage change	11.2		28.2	
Absolute change	.10		.70	

NOTES: People with zero or negative earnings were assigned earnings of $100 for variance of logs calculations (zero otherwise). CUR is equal to total labor earnings divided by earnings capacity without the variance adjustment. Earnings and earnings capacity are top-coded at $99,999 in 1988 dollars. Observations weighted using March supplemental weights.
SOURCE: Author's calculations using March 1974 and 1989 CPS.

1987 period.) Table 4–2 also indicates that the EC distribution grew more unequal.[18]

The ratio of individual earnings to EC for each observation can be considered a capacity utilization ratio (CUR). The distributions of CUR in 1973 and 1988 reveal the change in the dispersion of capacity utilization patterns over the fifteen-year period. Table 4–3 presents the VLN of the distribution of CUR, for workers and all males, for 1973 and 1988. The *dispersion* in capacity utilization increased substantially from 1973 to 1988. For workers the VLN of the distribution of capacity utilization rates increased by 11 percent; for all males a 28 percent increase is recorded.[19]

Knowing the distributions of earnings, EC and CUR, we can pursue a variant of the studies described earlier. Those studies decomposed the increased inequality in earnings into the change in dispersion of wage rates (interpreted as the distribution of opportunities) and changes in the dispersion of hours worked (interpreted as the distribution of voluntary choices).

By construction, annual earnings equals the product of EC and the capacity utilization rate, in much the same way that, in the earlier studies, earnings equaled the product of the wage rate and hours worked. Thus the decomposition property of the VLN measure of inequality is: $var(e) = var(ec) + var(cur) + 2cov(ec,cur)$.

From the estimates discussed above, we have a value of earnings and an estimated value of EC for each individual in our two samples. Hence we can construct estimates of the VLN of the distributions of two of the four terms in the above equation. By combining the final two terms in the equation [$var(cur)$ and $2cov(ec,cur)$] into a single term, we can decompose the increase in inequality in earnings into two parts. They are (1) the increase in inequality in EC; and (2) the change in the sum of $var(cur)$ and $2cov(ec,cur)$.[20]

Table 4–4 presents the results of this decomposition. The numbers in the first column indicate the level of the VLN of earnings in both 1973 and 1988 for working-age males with positive earnings. The VLN of earnings increased by .18 between those two years, an increase of 16.2 percent.

The next two columns show the components of this change—the change in the VLN of EC and the change in the sum of the combined VLNs of the two remaining terms in the equation. The VLN of EC increased from .28 to .35 (see table 4–2), an absolute increase of .07. A larger absolute change, however, is recorded for the sum of the VLNs of the two remaining terms, shown in the third column. This sum of VLNs increased by .11. The sum of the changes in the second and third columns (.07 + .11) is .18, the value of the absolute change in the VLN of earnings, shown as the first column.

For the sample of workers, then, the bulk of the increase in earnings inequality (as measured by the VLN of earnings)—about 63 percent—is attributable to the increase in dispersion of the CUR (plus the covariance

TABLE 4–4
SOURCE OF CHANGE IN THE VARIANCE OF LOG EARNINGS, MALE WORKERS AND ALL MALES AGED 18–64, 1973 AND 1988

	Variance of Log Earnings		Variance of Log Earnings Capacity		Sum of Variances of Log of CUR and Covariance Term
Male workers					
1973	1.110	=	.283	+	.826
1988	1.289	=	.349	+	.939
Absolute change	.179	=	.066	+	.113
Percentage of row total	100	=	36.9	+	63.1
All males					
1973	2.771	=	.288	+	2.484
1988	3.555	=	.353	+	3.203
Absolute change	.784	=	.065	+	.719
Percentage of row total	100	=	8.3	+	91.7

NOTES: People with zero or negative earnings were assigned earnings of $100 for variance of logs of earnings and CUR calculations (zero otherwise). Earnings capacity has variance adjustment. Observations weighted using March supplemental weights. Numbers may not add exactly across columns because of rounding.
SOURCE: Author's calculations using March 1974 and 1989 CPS.

term); only about 37 percent is attributable to the increase in the inequality of EC. The latter of these two terms—the changing inequality in EC—is properly interpreted as the increased dispersion of the potential services of human capital, or earnings capabilities, among workers. The effect of changes in inequality in earnings capabilities is less than the increase in the inequality in the rate of use of earnings capabilities. I conclude that at least half of the observed increase in earnings inequality among working males is attributable to increases in inequality in the utilization of earnings capabilities; about 40 percent is attributable to increases in inequality in the holding of earnings potential.[21]

Table 4–4 also presents the same calculation for all males, a group that includes those without earnings or work time. Because of the growth in the number of jobless working-age males over the 1973–1988 period, together with the rapid fall-off in the utilization of EC by those with low levels of EC, the result here is even more striking. More than 90 percent of the increased earnings inequality among all males (.784) is accounted for by increases in the sum of the VLN of the CUR and covariance term; less than 10 percent is attributable to the increase in inequality of human capital—EC.[22]

What, then, do I conclude from this exercise?

• First, the change in earnings inequality and its determinants differs sharply between male workers and all males of working age. The increase in inequality in both earnings and the CUR over the 1973–1988 period is substantially larger for the entire population of working-age males than it is for workers. This result is not surprising, considering the rapid absolute and relative increases over the period in the number of working-age males who reported neither working nor earning. It does, however, cast doubt on the legitimacy of relying only on samples of males who work to reach conclusions about the level of and change in earnings inequality among working-age males, and of the factors accounting for both the extent of inequality and the change in inequality.

• Second, the increase in earnings inequality over the 1973–1988 period has been decomposed in a manner analogous to decompositions found elsewhere in the literature.[23] These studies (see table 3–1) suggest that the change in wage rate inequality—often interpreted as a change in "opportunities"—has accounted for most, if not all, of the increase in earnings inequality since the early 1970s. The results presented here suggest that the change in inequality in the distribution of EC—which distribution is an analog to the wage rate—plays a far smaller role in explaining the increase in earnings inequality than others have attributed to changes in observed wage rate inequality. It follows that the choice of work hours (or the utilization of earnings capacity) may play a larger role than is commonly believed.

Two factors are relevant in attempting to account for this difference in results. Previous studies take estimates of observed wage rates as reflecting work and earnings opportunities. We assume that predicted FTYR earnings—which are equivalent to the FTYR wage rate—reflect earnings opportunities. Our earnings capacity measure recognizes that some workers may voluntarily trade off higher wages for nonpecuniary characteristics of a less-than-FTYR job (such as fewer or flexible work hours, proximity to residence, and less stress or difficulty) and seeks to purge the observed wage rate of these choices. A portion of the difference in results therefore stems from changes over time in the distributions of wage rates of individuals in the FTYR market and wage rates in the less-than-FTYR market.[24]

A second factor that may explain the difference stems from the noisy and precarious wage rate measure used in prior studies. Bound and others (1989) found that when wage rates are estimated by dividing annual earnings by the product of usual hours worked per week and the number of weeks worked, the measurement error is larger than for earnings and hours. Moreover, before 1976 the CPS data employed by these studies had only broad categorical information available on the number of weeks worked in the year and the number of hours worked in the week, and this may increase the measurement error even more. Because of the tenuous reliability of estimates based on such wage rates, we have employed a method that depends only on the reporting of annual earnings and whether the person worked FTYR.

5
The Sensitivity of Results to Beginning and Ending Dates

T he findings reported here provide evidence of changes in earnings inequality—and in the factors that may have determined these changes—between two points in time, typically a starting date early in the 1970s and an ending date of 1988. To the extent that these dates represent different points in the business cycle, the results may be an artifact of the beginning and ending dates chosen.

Table 5–1 presents summary results for both the EC/utilization and the wage rate/hours methods of decomposing the contribution of sources of earnings inequality. Two of the years in the period are cyclical peaks (1973, 1988) and two years are cyclical troughs (1975, 1991). The table shows calculations for male *workers.*

Over the entire 1973–1991 period, the VLN of earnings increased by .19 (from 1.11 to 1.30) (column 1). Over the same period, inequality in imputed FTYR wage rates (EC) increased by .08 (from .28 to .36) (column 2). Hence, the change in the inequality of EC was 41 percent of the increase in earnings inequality. Indeed, if the terminal year were 1988 rather than 1991, the change in EC inequality would account for 37 percent of the increase in earnings inequality. These results are consistent with the results presented earlier.

The calculations reported beneath these time trends suggest the sensitivity of calculations of the contribution

TABLE 5–1
VARIANCE OF LOGARITHM (VLN) OF EARNINGS, EARNINGS
CAPACITY, AND WAGE RATES, FOR MALE WORKERS AGED 18–64,
1973–1991

	(1) VLN Earnings	(2) VLN EC	(3) VLN Wage Rates
1973 (peak)	1.11	.28	(.70)
1975 (trough)	1.18	.27	.62
1988 (peak)	1.29	.35	.78
1991 (trough)	1.30	.36	.70

	Δ VLN EC / Δ VLN Earnings (%)	Δ VLN Wage Rates / Δ VLN Earnings (%)
1973–1988	+37	(+45)
1973–1991	+41	(+5)
1975–1988	+74	+109
1975–1991	+77	+63

NOTES: Wages are equal to: (annual earnings) / (weeks worked *
usual hours worked per week). For 1973, weeks worked are the
midpoint of the categorical weeks-worked variable, and hours
worked per week are taken from information on survey week (for
the people who did not work in survey week, full-time workers are
assigned forty hours and part-time workers twenty hours). Sample
includes all civilian males aged eighteen to sixty-four with positive
total earnings. Earnings and EC top-coded at $99,999 in 1991 dol-
lars. Estimates in parentheses indicate lack of comparable hours
and weeks-worked variables.
SOURCE: Data are from March CPS surveys from 1974, 1976, 1989,
and 1992.

of the *change* in EC inequality to the *change* in earnings
inequality to the initial and terminal year chosen for
analysis. Beginning the analysis in 1975 indicates that
growing inequality in EC accounted for about 75 percent
of the increase in earnings inequality, irrespective of the
terminal year. This result is consistent with the results
of the earlier studies shown in table 3–1. I conclude that

at least part of the difference in the conclusion reached in using my alternative decomposition of earnings inequality relative to that of the earlier studies may be due to differences in initial or terminal years of the analyses.

This conclusion seems even more valid when the analysis is performed using actual wage rates of male workers (column 3) rather than EC. Whereas the increase in the VLN of earnings from 1973 to 1991 was .19, the VLN of actual wage rates increased by .08 over the 1973–1988 period, by .16 over the 1975–1988 period, and by less than .01 over the entire 1973–1991 period. Beginning the analysis in 1975 suggests that the increase in wage rates accounts for at least two-thirds and perhaps as much as 100 percent of the increase in earnings inequality. Performing the same analysis from 1973 to the end of the 1980s, however, suggests that the increase in the VLN of wage rates could account for from virtually none of the increase in male earnings to nearly half the increase. Indeed, using actual wage rates rather than EC as the basis of analysis points out even more starkly the sensitivity of conclusions to the choice of the initial and terminal year of the analysis.

From these tabulations, I conclude that a convincing answer to the question of the contribution of the growth of wage rate inequality (reflecting changed opportunities) to the growth of earnings inequality is yet to be provided. Studies using both EC (based on imputed FTYR wage rates) and actual wage rates suggest that the conventional wisdom of the literature—namely, that the growth in male earnings inequality has been driven by growth in wage rate inequality and not by growth in work-time inequality (hours per year worked)—may be an artifact of both the unreliable nature of the wage rate used in the earlier studies and the choice of the initial and terminal dates of the analyses.[25]

6
Explaining the Increase in Earnings Inequality

At several points in this discussion of the relative contributions of changes in opportunities and choices to the rise in earnings inequality, I have alluded to the shift in work patterns from FTYR employment toward either joblessness or other categories of less-than-FTYR employment. If these shifts can be interpreted as largely reflecting choices about working time by male workers, they would call into doubt prior estimates of the overwhelming dominance of growing inequality in wage rates (opportunities) in explaining the growth in earnings inequality. These shifts in work-time patterns, again interpreted as reflecting voluntary choices, also support the conclusion of a large potential contribution of growing inequality in the utilization of earnings capabilities (the allocation decisions that lead individuals to work part-year, part-time, or not at all) in explaining the growth in earnings inequality.

In this chapter, I explore the changes in work patterns over the 1973 to 1988 period in an effort to see whether the changes help explain the relative contributions of opportunity and choice to the growth of earnings inequality. I attempt to answer two questions:

- Within standard categories of male work patterns, what has been the profile of changes over time in wage rate and work-time variability?
- What has been the effect of changes in the structure

TABLE 6-1
ALLOCATION OF ALL MALES AND WORKERS AGED 18–64 ACROSS
WORK PATTERN CATEGORIES, 1973–1991
(percent)

	FTYR	FTPY	PTYR	PTPY	No Work	Total
All males						
1973 (peak)	66.8	18.4	2.7	4.7	7.4	100.0
1975 (trough)	59.9	22.2	2.7	4.7	10.5	100.0
1988 (peak)	64.7	15.8	3.1	5.4	11.0	100.0
1991 (trough)	60.5	17.5	3.6	5.7	12.7	100.0
	FTYR	FTPY	PTYR	PTPY		Total
Workers						
1973 (peak)	72.3	19.9	2.8	5.1		100.0
1975 (trough)	67.0	24.8	3.0	5.3		100.0
1988 (peak)	72.7	17.7	3.5	6.0		100.0
1991 (trough)	69.3	20.1	4.1	6.6		100.0

NOTES: Self-employed workers are excluded from this sample. FTYR = full time, year round; FTPY = full time, part year; PTYR = part time, year round; PTPY = part time, part year.
SOURCE: Author's calculations using March 1974, 1976, 1989, and 1992 CPS.

of male work patterns—as between, say, full-time, year-round work and part-time or part-year work—on the changing pattern of earnings inequality?

Table 6–1 shows the allocation of both all males and male workers in different categories of work patterns and reveals two important changes over the period 1973–1991. First, there was a substantial increase in joblessness among working-age males—from 7.4 percent to nearly 13 percent. The increase is even larger in absolute terms; in 1973 there were about 3.5 million jobless working-age males, but by 1991 the number of jobless had grown to 8.4 million. This change in the prevalence of joblessness contributes to the difference in the perception of the level of and changes in earnings inequality between male workers and all males and in the relative contributions of changes in EC and wage rate inequality to increased earnings inequality.

Second, there was also a substantial increase in the prevalence of part-time work, among both year-round and part-year workers. In 1973 about 8 percent of working males were employed part time; by 1991 the figure was nearly 11 percent. Whereas in 1973 about 13 percent of all working-age males were either not working or working part time (7.1 million persons), by 1991, 22 percent of all males (14.6 million) were either jobless or working part time.

Table 6–2 summarizes several patterns and trends in inequality in earnings, wage rates, and hours worked in the various full- and part-time categories identified. The most important patterns are as follows:

• The growth in earnings inequality among FTYR workers is substantial, and within that category the increase in wage rate inequality accounts for the bulk of the growth in earnings inequality.

• The level of earnings inequality is substantially larger in the non-FTYR work categories than in the FTYR category, and (with the exception of the PTYR category) inequality in hours accounts for much of the variance in earnings. There was no substantial growth in earnings inequality in the non-FTYR categories.

• From this, it follows that the increase in the share of working-age males who are not working FTYR may contribute to our understanding of the sources of the growth in earnings inequality among workers. This increase can be thought of as a shift of working-age males from FTYR work (with low earnings inequality) to part-time and part-year work (with substantially higher earnings inequality). If this is so, the conventional wisdom attributing the dominance of growing wage rate inequality in explaining the growth of male earnings inequality may camouflage the fact that an important source of the real increase in earnings inequality is the shift away from FTYR work.

TABLE 6-2
VARIANCE OF LOGARITHM (VLN) OF EARNINGS, WAGE RATES, AND HOURS, ALL MALES AND WORKERS AGED 18–64, ACROSS WORK PATTERN CATEGORIES, 1973–1991

	(1) FTYR	(2) FTPY	(3) PTYR	(4) PTPY	(5) Total Workers	(6) Total Males
1973[a]						
VLN earnings	.36	1.15	1.36	1.64	.96	2.90
VLN wage rates	(.35)	(.61)	(.88)	(1.08)	(.48)	(.90)
VLN hours	(.12)	(.48)	(1.87)	(1.20)	(.48)	(4.29)
VLN wage rate/VLN earnings					(.50)	(.31)
VLN hours/VLN earnings					(.50)	(1.48)
1975						
VLN earnings	.30	1.05	.76	1.52	1.03	3.52
VLN wage rates	.30	.47	.67	.67	.42	.94
VLN hours	.02	.48	.20	1.09	.43	5.56
VLN wage rate/VLN earnings					.41	.27
VLN hours/VLN earnings					.42	1.58

(Table continues)

33

TABLE 6–2 (continued)

	(1) FTYR	(2) FTPY	(3) PTYR	(4) PTPY	(5) Total Workers	(6) Total Males
1988						
VLN earnings	.40	1.16	.89	1.68	1.13	3.76
VLN wage rates	.37	.57	.79	.77	.50	1.02
VLN hours	.05	.45	.18	1.02	.40	5.85
VLN wage rate/VLN earnings					.44	.27
VLN hours/VLN earnings					.35	1.56
1991						
VLN earnings	.40	1.08	.69	1.72	1.15	4.01
VLN wage rates	.37	.56	.62	.69	.50	1.06
VLN hours	.02	.42	.15	1.16	.43	6.51
VLN wage rate/VLN earnings					.43	.26
VLN hours/VLN earnings					.37	1.62

NOTE: Self-employed workers are excluded from this sample.
a. Estimates for 1973 are in parentheses because of lack of comparable hours and weeks-worked variables. See note, table 4–1.
SOURCE: Author's calculations using March 1974, 1976, 1989, and 1992 CPS.

7
Increased Earnings Inequality and Changes in Work Patterns

I n this chapter I examine the contribution of changing work patterns—viewed as reflecting largely voluntary choices—to the increase in earnings inequality from 1975 to 1991. I ask the question, How much would earnings inequality have increased over this period if the distribution of earnings in the work pattern categories remained at 1975 levels but the proportion of the population in those categories reflected the 1991 distribution?

I assume that mean earnings and earnings inequality in work pattern categories remains constant (at some base level) and that only the *share* of workers in each work pattern category changes. That is, I decompose the change in inequality into two components: (1) the change that is due to changes in work patterns; and (2) the change that is due to changes in mean incomes across groups and to changes in inequality within groups.

This decomposition is shown in table 7–1 for workers and for all males, again using the VLN measure of inequality.[26] Although these decompositions fail to reflect changes in mean income or inequality that are due to changes in the composition of the groups, they do provide relevant information and tell a consistent story—namely, that changes in the allocation of males across the work-pattern categories have contributed substantially to the

TABLE 7-1
Change in Inequality Accounted for by Changes in Work Pattern Categories for Civilian, Male, Wage and Salary Workers and All Civilian Males Aged 18 to 64, 1975–1991

	Actual	Variance of Log Earnings (VLN)	
		1975 group means and group inequality	1991 group means and group inequality
Male workers			
1975	1.03	1.03	1.12
1991	1.16	1.07	1.16
Absolute change	.13	.04	.04
Percentage of actual change accounted for by change in work pattern categories		31	31
All males			
1975	3.52	3.52	3.55
1991	4.01	3.99	4.01
Absolute change	.49	.47	.46
Percentage of actual change accounted for by change in work pattern categories		96	94

NOTE: Self-employed workers are excluded from this sample. Nonworkers are assigned $100 for VLN calculations.
SOURCE: Author's calculations using March 1976 and 1992 CPS.

increase in male earnings inequality. These reallocations increased the share of the population in work categories with very high and very low (or zero) levels of mean earnings, thus increasing the between-group variance of earnings (see table 6–1). In addition, the changed allocations resulted in an increased concentration of males in the high-variation, part-time work categories (see table 6–2). In general, changing work patterns accounted for about one-third of the increase in inequality among workers and about 95 percent of the increase in inequality for the sample of all working-age males.[27] These changing work patterns would appear to solve part of the puzzle of whether wage rate or work time ("opportunities" versus "choices") contributes more to increased earnings inequality; changes in work patterns that to a large extent reflect voluntary choices may account for a sizable share of the increase in earnings inequality.

8
Conclusion

This effort to shed light on the relative roles of changes in opportunities and choices in the growth in earnings inequality over the past two decades has rested on two distinct factors: (1) the relative contributions of changes in the inequality of human capital (or earnings capability, viewed as reflecting opportunity); and (2) changes in the utilization of earnings capability (viewed as reflecting work-effort choices). I conclude that:

- The increase in inequality in both earnings and the utilization of earnings capacity over the 1973–1988 period is substantially larger for the entire population of working-age males than it is for workers. This difference casts doubt on the legitimacy of relying only on samples of males who work to reach conclusions about the level of and changes in earnings inequality among working-age males.

- These estimates of the level of and changes in inequality in the distribution of the potential services of human capital—earnings capacity (EC)—suggest that the change in inequality in this analog to the wage rate (a proxy for inequality in the distribution of opportunities offered workers by the labor market) plays a far smaller role in explaining the increase in earnings inequality than others have attributed to changes in observed wage rate inequality (see table 3–1). It follows that the choice of work hours (or the utilization of earnings capacity) may play a larger role than is commonly believed.

Moreover, from the calculations presented here on the issue of whether changes in work-time inequality—as reflected in shifts in workers across work categories—can account for the increase in earnings inequality over the past two decades, I conclude that changes in the allocation of males across work-pattern categories reveal underlying inequality developments that are camouflaged in more aggregate calculations. These changes have contributed substantially to the increase in male earnings inequality in two ways: by increasing the share of the population in work categories with very high or very low levels of mean earnings (thus increasing the size of the between-group variance) and by increasing the concentration of males in the high-variation, part-time work categories.

These findings shed light on the contribution of work time and wage rate to increased earnings inequality and cast doubt on the conventional view that voluntary choice plays little or no role. Although they do not resolve the issue of the role of choice and opportunity in explaining the increase in male earnings inequality, they suggest that the choice-versus-opportunity puzzle is more complex than the conventional wisdom would have us believe.

What implications for public discussion and policy do these results and this conclusion carry with them? First, and perhaps most important, is their effect on our perceptions of how serious a social problem is implied by the increased earnings inequality among men of working age. The extent of concern is clearly a positive function of one's assessment of the involuntary nature of the change that workers have experienced. The smaller the potential role of involuntary factors—or the greater the role of voluntary choices—the less urgent and immediate the problem seems.

Second, although it is plausible that voluntary choices account for a bigger share of the increase in male earnings inequality than previously believed, that voluntary choice is a large factor in explaining the increase in family income inequality or family poverty is far less plausible. The factors that determine this distribution include changes in family structure, spousal work patterns, and family size, and they are even more complex than those that determine male earnings inequality.

Third, it seems likely that, to some important extent, what I have described as voluntary choice reflects changes in people's tastes for work and leisure, or changes in policy-induced incentives to the labor supply. Changes in both tastes and nonwork income opportunities would seem relevant in understanding the increase in retirement and partial retirement before the standard retirement age. And surely one could not rule out taste changes in understanding the reduction in the propensity to work at all on the part of youths with little education.

Changes in tastes are difficult for economists to deal with, but we do know that changes in economic incentives can be employed to counter changes in tastes. This consideration strengthens the case for a wage-rate subsidy targeted at low-wage workers as a means of reducing the increase in nonwork, or to stem the trend toward part-time work. Conversely, it weakens the case for reducing earnings or income inequality through increases in public transfers that are not conditioned on work. Both conclusions argue for making public income support to the able-bodied and those not otherwise constrained from working contingent on their providing some socially productive effort.

Notes

1. A commonly used technique for decomposing changes in earnings inequality into changes in wage rate inequality and changes in work-time inequality is based on an accounting property of the variance of the natural logarithm (VLN) measure of inequality. Relying on this property, an accounting definition of the components of the VLN of earnings [$var(e)$] is: $var(e) = var(h) + var(w) + 2cov(h,w)$. From microdata, values of earnings, wage rates, and hours worked can be obtained for each individual in a national sample. For two samples of the same population observed at different points in time, estimates of the $var(e)$, $var(w)$, and $var(h)$ can be obtained. With these values for each of the two years, the change in the inequality of earnings [$var(e)$] between the two years can be decomposed into the change in the inequality of wage rates [$var(w)$] and the change in the inequality of work time [$var(h)$], plus the covariance term.

2. Following this logic, if the distribution of wage *rates*—taken to describe the structure of opportunities—shows no increase in its dispersion from t to $t + 1$, any observed increase in the inequality of earnings over this period must reflect an increase in the variation of hours worked—taken to reflect a change in the work-time choice.

3. The residual, or covariance term, in the empirical procedure is assumed to be zero in these examples.

4. Details of Burtless's sample and the samples used in other studies discussed in this section can be found in the notes to table 3–1.

5. Bound and others (1989) find that the measurement error for hourly wages from the CPS is much greater than measurement error for annual earnings. Burtless acknowledges the weakness of the hourly wage data, and indicates that the awkward procedures necessary to calculate this variable "may cause serious errors in estimating the variance of wage rates." He notes that because of this measurement procedure "some of the variability in annual earnings that ought properly to be attributed to hours will be attributed to wage rates instead" (Burtless 1990, p. 110).

6. Annual hours were estimated by the product of survey work hours and the estimate of weeks worked in the prior year. The weeks-worked variable is, in turn, estimated by the midpoint of the weeks worked category in 1973 and an equivalent midpoint assignment from the continuous weeks worked variable in 1987. Annual reported earnings, then, are divided by the hours worked variable, so estimated, in calculating the wage rate. Hence, the distribution of the wage rate and the hours worked variables is affected by the precarious procedure for estimating the annual hours variable. From his table 1 (p. 203), the VLN of earnings for white males increases from 1.116 to 1.267 over the 1973 to 1987 period, an increase of .151. From his table 7 (p. 216), the VLN of his estimate of hourly wages increases from .700 in 1973 to .910 in 1987, an increase of .210. The same table reveals that the VLN of estimated hours worked changes from .619 to .544, a *decrease* of .075. These values suggest the unlikely conclusion that the increase in inequality of hourly wage rates from 1973 to 1987 was about 140 percent of the increase in inequality of earnings. They also suggest that, in spite of the substantial increase in the incidence of part-time and part-year work over this period (see Blank [1990]), inequality in work time (annual hours of work) actually *fell*.

7. Two other studies rely on FTYR workers to shed light on the changes in inequality of earnings. One is by Juhn, Murphy, and Pierce (1989); the other is by Blackburn (1990). By limiting their samples to FTYR workers, they largely purge their earnings variable of the influence of variability in work time. The calculations of Juhn, Murphy, and Pierce

indicate that the VLN measure of inequality rose from .50 to .59 between 1973 and 1985, an increase of .09. Blackburn finds the VLN of annual earnings for working-age white males rose from .25 in 1973 to .32 in 1985, an increase of .07.

8. For example, the larger increase in the VLN of the wage rate of all workers, relative to that of FTYR workers, has no obvious explanation. Could it be that workers—either those changing jobs or those entering the labor force—are being offered, or are choosing, part-time and part-year jobs (see Blank 1990), or jobs with hourly pay rates that are substantially below the mean, which could lead to this result? Or could it reflect the popular impression that many workers' real wages are declining, and that many are working harder and more hours in order to avoid reductions in real earnings?

9. This section and the next draw on Haveman and Buron 1994a.

10. This estimate of the "jobless" includes, among others, those who have retired before the normal retirement age, full-time students with no paid employment over the year, and those who are unemployed for the entire year.

11. Hence, the inequality in the distribution of both w and h is a reflection of the distribution of perceived worker needs, tastes, and circumstances at that time. In addition, the distributions of w and h reflect the structure of wages and hours offered by employers. Because w and h are subject both to exogenous shocks and to changing needs, tastes, technologies, and opportunities, both are short-run and transitory variables.

12. This would be the case if the distributions of offered and desired work times, implicit prices of human capital characteristics, wage offers, and tastes were constant over time.

13. The change in the utilization of human capital could be due to either changing tastes or changing work-time offers. The opposite result could occur if the underlying distributions of human capital characteristics, their implicit prices, wage offers, and tastes were held constant.

14. I assume that the implicit price paid to human capi-

tal characteristics would remain the same if everyone worked full time, year round.

15. Full-time, year-round workers are a select sample of working-age males, in that they have special characteristics that lead to their working at capacity. If these characteristics are not adjusted for by means of a selectivity correction, the value of EC imputed to other working-age males from the estimated earnings equations would assume that they had the same characteristics as the FTYR workers. These imputed values would therefore be biased.

16. When forming the distribution of EC for the population, I adjusted the expected (or predicted) EC value for each individual to account for unobserved variables in the earnings-generation process; I refer to these estimates as "variance-adjusted EC." This process allows one to obtain a distribution of individual EC that reflects both the human capital characteristics of the population of working-age males in 1973 and 1988 and the implicit "prices" attached to those characteristics in each year.

17. Table 4–2 also indicates that inequality in EC as a proportion of earnings inequality increased between 1973 and 1988, suggesting that the contribution of the *increase* in earnings capacity inequality to the increase in earnings inequality over the period exceeded the average contribution of earnings capacity inequality to earnings inequality. A similar finding, but for wages rather than EC, was reported by Moffitt (1990). For white males, Moffitt reported that the VLN of wages in 1973 was 62 percent of the VLN of earnings, and that this percentage rose to 72 by 1987. For blacks, however, the VLN of the wage rate as a percentage of the VLN of earnings *fell* from 62 percent to 56 percent over the same period.

18. In *percentage* terms, the level of inequality of EC increased by more than the level of inequality of earnings for workers; for all males, the percentage increase in inequality of EC was somewhat less than the percentage increase in inequality of earnings. For both workers and all males, however, the *absolute* increase in the inequality of earnings was substantially larger than the increase in the inequality of EC. It follows from this that the increase in the inequality

of earnings capacity contributed to the increase in earnings inequality, but that an increase in the dispersion of hours worked (or the "utilization of earnings capacity") also contributed to the increased earnings dispersion.

19. For both the male workers and all males, individuals with low EC tended to use far less of their human capital than men with higher earnings potential. For all males, for example, the mean CUR was about two-thirds in both years; the CUR at low levels of EC is generally less than .5. Moreover, at very low levels of EC, the CUR fell substantially over the 1973–1988 period. The mean CUR of individuals in the bottom quintile of the distribution was .53 in 1973; by 1988 it had fallen by 12 percent, to .47. This decrease suggests a growing incidence of less-than-FTYR work for individuals with low earnings capacity, an issue to which I will return.

20. It should be noted that the value of the CUR for individuals is the ratio of the observed value of earnings and the estimated value of EC, and therefore is not based on an independent estimate. As a result, because the covariance term does not have an unambiguous interpretation in this decomposition, the CUR and covariance term are treated as one in the results reported below.

21. These results concerning the relative contributions of (1) the change in the inequality of earnings capabilities; and (2) the change in the inequality with which these capabilities are used to the change in earnings inequality are suggestive rather than definitive. The estimates in table 4–4 reflect the distribution of earnings capabilities constructed from predicted earnings (from selectivity-corrected earnings regressions), adjusted by a standard error. This adjustment was necessary to correct for the artificial compression of the variance of the distribution of earnings capabilities based on predicted values from estimated regression coefficients. The standard error employed is the estimated standard error of the residual from the regressions. This procedure assumes that the residual standard error appropriate for all workers (and all males) is that estimated for FTYR workers.

Because this assumption is implicitly inconsistent with the selectivity-corrected model, I also calculated the standard error of the residual of the unobserved distribution of FTYR earnings offers. This residual is unobserved because not all workers (or all males) are employed full-time, year round. When the standard error from this distribution—unobserved, but consistent with the model—is used in the adjustment, the change in the inequality of worker earnings attributable to the change in the inequality of their earnings capacity *falls to about 10 percent.*

I also estimated the effect of the change in earnings capacity inequality on the change in earnings inequality using the distribution of predicted earnings capacity values (that is, with no adjustment) and found a contribution of about 20 percent. Finally, I estimated the model without the correction for selectivity into FTYR work and found that the change in earnings capacity inequality accounted for nearly 30 percent of the change in worker earnings inequality.

Hence, the contribution of the change in the inequality of EC to the change in the inequality of earnings described in the text is larger than these alternative estimates.

22. The calculations for the sample of all males replaces observations of zero earnings for the jobless with a value of $100. The overall conclusion is not sensitive to this assumption. Were $1 used in place of $100, only about 3 percent of the increase in the inequality of earnings among all males would be attributed to the increase in EC inequality. Substituting $300 for $100 yields an estimate of about 12 percent.

23. As emphasized earlier, in these studies changes in inequality in the observed wage rates of workers are taken as the measure of changes in inequality in the price of labor, or of "opportunities"; changes in inequality in hours worked per year are taken as the measure of changes in inequality in workers' "choices" about the quantity of labor they will supply.

24. Clearly, some workers who wish to work FTYR do not have the opportunity. Although the difference in the wage rates they receive in the part-time or part-year market and their FTYR wage rate may reflect opportunities, this difference is included in our capacity utilization term and is taken to reflect "choice." Thus, while studies that rely on observed wage rates attribute to opportunity factors that may repre-

sent choices, our estimates may attribute to choice some factors that reflect opportunities. It follows that studies that rely on observed wage rates tend to exaggerate the contribution of opportunity to earnings inequality, while this one may tend to understate the role of opportunity.

25. A comparable analysis for all males, rather than male workers, found the same sort of sensitivity to starting and ending dates.

26. The VLN decomposition is based on the formula in Allison 1978.

27. For the sample of males with positive earnings, the decomposition of the increase in inequality into the component due to the changing share of workers in FTYR, FTPY, PTYR, and PTPY work categories and the component due to changes in mean earnings and inequality in work-time categories is reported in table 7–1. Column 1 shows that the actual VLN of earnings increased from 1.03 to 1.16 from 1975 to 1991. Column 2 shows that if group means and inequality are held at the 1975 levels but the share of workers in each group is allowed to change to reflect actual changes, then the VLN of earnings would only have increased from 1.03 to 1.07. Column 3 shows that if group means and inequality are held constant at 1991 levels, the VLN of earnings would have been 1.12 in 1975 and 1.16 in 1991. In both cases, 31 percent of the increase in inequality is attributed to changes in the share of workers across work-time categories. For all males, the VLN of earnings increased from 3.52 to 4.01 from 1975 to 1991. About 95 percent of this change is attributed to the changing distribution of workers across work-time categories. Changing patterns of work explain more of the increase in inequality for all males than for male workers because of the increasing number of nonworkers. The percentage of nonworkers increased from 10.5 percent of the male population in 1975 to 12.7 percent in 1991.

References

Allison, Paul D. 1978. "Measures of Inequality." *American Sociological Review* 43(6): 865–80.

Blackburn, McKinley. 1990. "What Can Explain the Increase in Earnings Inequality among Males?" *Industrial Relations* 29(3): 441–56.

Blank, Rebecca M. 1990. "Are Part-Time Jobs Bad Jobs?" In *A Future of Lousy Jobs*, ed. Gary Burtless. Washington, D.C.: Brookings Institution.

Bluestone, Barry. 1989. "The Changing Nature of Employment and Earnings in the U.S. Economy: 1963–1987." Paper prepared for the conference "Job Creation in America," University of North Carolina at Chapel Hill, April 10, 1989.

Bound, John, Charles Brown, Greg J. Duncan, and Willard L. Rodgers. 1989. "Measurement Error in Cross-Sectional and Longitudinal Labor Market Surveys: Results from Two Validation Studies." National Bureau of Economic Research Working Paper #2884. Cambridge, Mass.

Burtless, Gary. 1990. "Earnings Inequality over the Business and Demographic Cycles." In *A Future of Lousy Jobs*, ed. Gary Burtless. Washington, D.C.: Brookings Institution.

Haveman, Robert, and Lawrence Buron. 1994a. "The Growth in Male Earnings Inequality, 1973–1988: The Role of Earnings Capacity and Utilization." In *The Changing Distribution of Income in an Open U.S.*

Economy, ed. J. H. Bergstrand, T. F. Cosimano, J. W. Houck, and R. G. Sheehan. Amsterdam (Netherlands): North-Holland.

————. 1994b. "The Anatomy of Changing Male Earnings Inequality: An Empirical Exploration of Determinants." Institute for Research on Poverty Discussion Paper, University of Wisconsin-Madison.

Juhn, Chinhui, Kevin M. Murphy, and Brooks Pierce. 1989. "Wage Inequality and the Rise in Returns to Skill." Paper presented at the Universities Research Conference "Labor Markets in the 1990s," November 13, 1989.

Karoly, Lynn A. 1992. "The Trend in Inequality among Families, Individuals, and Workers in the U.S.: A Twenty-Five-Year Perspective." Rand Corporation # R-4206-rc. Santa Monica, Calif.

Levy, Frank, and Richard J. Murnane. 1992. "U.S. Earnings Levels and Earnings Inequality: A Review of Recent Trends and Proposed Explanations." *Journal of Economic Literature* 30(3): 1333–81.

Moffitt, Robert A. 1990. "The Distribution of Earnings and the Welfare State." In *A Future of Lousy Jobs*, ed. Gary Burtless. Washington, D.C.: Brookings Institution.

About the Author

ROBERT H. HAVEMAN is the John Bascom Professor of Economics and Public Policy, Department of Economics and Robert M. LaFollette Institute of Public Affairs, and a research affiliate in the Institute for Research on Poverty at the University of Wisconsin-Madison. Before 1970, he was professor of economics at Grinnell College; senior economist at the Joint Economic Committee, U.S. Congress; and research professor at the Brookings Institution. Mr. Haveman was the director of the Institute for Research on Poverty from 1970 to 1975, and he has served as a fellow at the Netherlands Institute for Advanced Study and as Tinbergen Professor at Erasmus University in the Netherlands.

He was the director of the Robert M. LaFollette Institute of Public Affairs from 1988 to 1991 and was coeditor of the *American Economic Review* from 1985 to 1991. Mr. Haveman's fields of interest include public finance, the economics of poverty, and social policy, including disability policy. His publications include *Earnings Capacity, Poverty, and Inequality* (1978); *Starting Even: An Equal Opportunity Program to Combat the Nation's New Poverty* (1988); and *Succeeding Generations: On the Effects of Investments in Children* (1994). He has also published in the *American Economic Review,* the *Review of Economics and Statistics,* and the *Quarterly Journal of Economics.*

AEI STUDIES ON UNDERSTANDING
ECONOMIC INEQUALITY
Marvin H. Kosters, series editor

THE DISTRIBUTION OF WEALTH: INCREASING INEQUALITY?
John C. Weicher

EARNINGS INEQUALITY: THE INFLUENCE OF CHANGING
OPPORTUNITIES AND CHOICES
Robert H. Haveman

INCOME MOBILITY AND THE MIDDLE CLASS
*Richard V. Burkhauser, Amy D. Crews, Mary C. Daly,
and Stephen P. Jenkins*

RELATIVE WAGE TRENDS, WOMEN'S WORK,
AND FAMILY INCOME
Chinhui Juhn

WAGE INEQUALITY: INTERNATIONAL COMPARISONS
OF ITS SOURCES
Francine D. Blau and Lawrence M. Kahn